# EP

659.36
3

# Rich and Poor Countries

## A study in problems
## of comparisons of real income

## DAN USHER

## EATON PAPER 9

# Rich and Poor Countries

## A study in problems
## of comparisons of real income

## DAN USHER

*Assistant Professor of Economics,*
*Graduate School of Business,*
*Columbia University, New York*

Published by

THE INSTITUTE OF ECONOMIC AFFAIRS

1966

First published October, 1966

© THE INSTITUTE OF ECONOMIC AFFAIRS LIMITED

*Printed in Great Britain by*

**IMPRESS (HEREFORD) LTD.**

Maylord Street · Hereford

# Foreword

The general purpose of the *Eaton Papers* is to contribute a stream of informative and analytical texts, drawing on the authors' researches, for specialist readers: teachers and students of economics, economists in business, nationalised industries and government, business managers, accountants, investment advisors, lawyers and others. The common theme is the sources and extent of economic information for business and public policy, the restrictions on it and methods of removing them, its scope, interpretation, reliability and limitations.

The better performance of an economy depends not only on increasing the amount of resources and their efficiency in existing uses but also on their better allocation between alternative uses on the basis of decisions made by consumers, firms, public authorities and governments. The quality of these decisions depends in large part on the accuracy and availability of relevant information.

The development of economic analysis has tended to ignore or underrate the costs of collecting and disseminating information, and the textbook analysis of competitive markets is usually based on the assumption that knowledge is perfect and costless. In a dynamic economy complete knowledge is unobtainable: *ex hypothesi* the conditions of supply and demand are continually changing, and the changes cannot be predicted with a high degree of accuracy because the future is in large part determined by events and decisions that in turn are influenced by information unknown and possibly unknowable in the present. Not least the collection and assimilation of information cost time, money and alternatives sacrificed that may outweigh its value.[1]

\* \* \*

Public policy, both internal and international, is necessarily based on estimates of relevant categories: measurement of the movement of retail and wholesale prices, wage rates, industrial production, national income, exports and imports. The debate on aid for developing countries draws on calculations of the incomes of rich and poor countries. If these estimates are substantially incorrect large errors in policy may be made.

In view of the large differences of judgement on the real incomes of the developing countries and on the gap between them and the rich countries, the

[1] Titles in the *Eaton Papers* series are listed on the back cover.

Institute invited Dr. Dan Usher, an economist who has specialised in the study and calculation of real incomes and their comparison, to write an appraisal of the problems confronted in measuring them. He has written an informed and penetrating analysis that not only students and teachers of economics but also people concerned with public policy should find enlightening and sobering. Dr. Usher demonstrates the technical problems of including elements of income that are part of real income but that cannot be assessed because they do not enter into the market, the difficulties in measuring and comparing movements in prices in different countries and the varying results given by different methods of measurement. Conclusions drawn from such tenuous calculations may be precarious.

The differences of measurement are graphically illustrated by the reflection that some countries with low incomes such as Afghanistan have never had a population census and that Nigeria and other countries have had to revise population estimates drastically; sometimes the revisions are upward, so that income per head was lower than supposed. Since population figures are used in estimating national products, these too are presumably suspect. Dr. Usher is concerned with the conceptual rather than the statistical differences of measuring real income. Analysis of the latter would presumably fortify the scepticism with which his analysis suggests the calculation must be regarded.

There are significant differences in the methods of measuring or reflecting satisfactions in developing and developed countries. Even in richer countries, as Professor Oskar Morgenstern has graphically shown,[1] the value of output, in total or per head, can be taken only very broadly as indicative of living standards. In the developing countries where markets are not highly developed there is not even a rough and ready measurement of real income.

Dr. Usher refers to the view that, beyond a point, further improvement in satisfaction consists in owning more than others. The relative conception of income, affluence or poverty is common in discussions of social policy in Britain. Dr. Usher's observation is of interest:

'It may be that when real income reaches a certain level further satisfaction consists only in having more than one's neighbour. Were this so, an increase in national incomes of rich countries distributed in proportion to present relative shares would make no-one better off'

This proposition may perhaps apply to some extent to rich and poor countries at present standards of living. The discussion of poverty as a relative concept may not be very illuminating since it is in effect a discussion of the distribution of income.

Dr. Usher refers to the unavoidable subjective element in the calculation

[1] *On the Accuracy of Economic Observations*, Second Edition, Princeton, 1963.

of real income. He observes that here 'the independent scholar has much more freedom than does the government statistician who, quite properly, must justify his figures by generally accepted statistical criteria'. His main conclusion is that 'the subject lies on the borderline between science and opinion. Careful reasoning and statistical technique can refine judgment and reduce the extent of subjectivity . . . but they cannot do away with subjectivity altogether'.

The Institute and the members of its Advisory Council do not necessarily share Dr. Usher's analysis or conclusions, but the Institute offers them as a scholarly analysis of the uncertainties of statistical calculation at a time when there is considerable public interest in living standards in rich and poor countries.

*July* 1966                                                           EDITOR

## The Author

DAN USHER, a Canadian, is an assistant professor of economics at the Graduate School of Business of Columbia University in New York City. After studying at McGill University and the University of Chicago, he worked for a time at the United Nations Economic Commission for Asia and the Far East in Bangkok, and he has recently been a Research Fellow at Nuffield College, Oxford.

# Contents

# I Introduction

Statistics of real national incomes of countries are intended as barometer-readings of prosperity. The scale of prosperity is graduated in units of money, for countries, like people, tend to record their economic well-being in this way. Thus national incomes of India and the United Kingdom may be compared in amounts of US dollars per head. The national income is defined as the yield of the economic system over the year including all consumption goods —food, clothing, services of houses, cars—all capital goods—new factories, new houses—and public administration. The word 'real' is placed in the phrase 'real national income' to indicate that national incomes are compared in a way that gives equal weight on the scale to equal amounts of the same commodity consumed in different places, just as economic growth in a single country is assessed not from the ratios of money national incomes at two periods of time but from this ratio corrected for changes in the cost of living.

The oldest, simplest and still most widely-used method of measuring real national income per head is that used by the United Nations in preparing its statistics of incomes in $ US per capita, presented here as Table I. The income figures in the Table were constructed by dividing the national incomes in local currencies by the populations and by the foreign exchange rates.[1] It is this Table in its complete form that is usually referred to in classification of countries as 'developed' or 'underdeveloped', 'rich' or 'poor'. Countries with incomes below a certain figure are classified as underdeveloped; countries with incomes above it as developed.

TABLE I

## ESTIMATES OF PER CAPITA GROSS DOMESTIC PRODUCTS IN US DOLLARS, 1963

| United States | 2,790 | Rhodesia | 139 |
| France | 1,406 | Thailand | 101 |
| United Kingdom | 1,361 | India | 76 |
| Argentina | 563 | Burma | 64 |
| Turkey | 230 | Ethiopia | 40 |

*Source: Yearbook of National Accounts Statistics 1964*, United Nations, Table 6A.

The justification for using the foreign exchange rate in computing real incomes is tied up with the doctrine known as purchasing power parity. The

[1] The national income of India in 1963 was 163 thousand million rupees, the population was 451 million and the foreign exchange rate was 4·76 rupees to the dollar.
Therefore the national income in $ US per capita was

$$\frac{163}{4\cdot76 \times 451} \text{ thousand}$$

equal to $76 per head per annum.

9

UK national income expressed in shillings is equal to the UK national income expressed in pounds divided by the exchange rate between shillings and pounds, and the exchange rate between shillings and pounds is, again by definition, equal to the UK cost of living in shillings divided by the UK cost of living in pounds. Similarly, according to the purchasing power parity doctrine, the real national income of India expressed in dollars is equal to the real national income of India expressed in rupees divided by the exchange rate between dollars and rupees, and the exchange rate between dollars and rupees is an indicator of comparative costs of living. The purchasing power parity doctrine implies that to compare incomes through the foreign exchange rate is equivalent to dividing each of the incomes by an index of the cost of living.

Unfortunately the purchasing power parity doctrine is not altogether true. It is near enough to the truth that statistics of national income per capita in $ US seem to place most countries in the right order on the scale of rich and poor, but the absolute magnitudes are very wrong and some important differences between countries fail to be reflected in the statistics.

Ethiopia is shown in the Table to have an income of $40 per capita per year; the average Ethiopian has an income of only 11 cents per day from which he must deduct a few cents for his share of government expenditure and investment before arriving at the amount he has available for consumption. What could this possibly mean? It is difficult to say what the cost of subsistence is in the United States but there is no doubt that it is well above 11c. per day. A man would starve if he had only 11c. a day in the United States. Ethiopians survive. Therefore either the income of Ethiopia is higher than $40 per capita per annum, or the figure of $40 must be reinterpreted in a way that does not carry the inferences about poverty and welfare that we are accustomed to associate with the figure.

There are two main reasons why the foreign exchange rate may differ significantly from the purchasing power parity.

(1) The official exchange rate may differ from the equilibrium rate required to keep a country's trade in balance. There is a range in which governments can peg their exchange rates high or low; and a country cannot be said to have a high national income merely because its government has fixed the exchange rate at a value higher than is warranted by the flow of trade.[1]

(2) A far more serious difficulty with these statistics is that even the equilibrium foreign exchange rate fails to reflect the purchasing power parity. There is

[1] The United Nations has remedied this defect by preparing alternative estimates of income at what it believes to be equilibrium rates of exchange between currencies. These corrections have not altered the figures significantly. The explanation of the low figures for the underdeveloped countries must be sought elsewhere.

reason to suppose that the bias is systematic; on converting all prices into $ US by the foreign exchange rate, it turns out that the price levels are lowest in the poorest countries. The lower the real standard of living, the greater the disparity between the exchange rate and comparative living cost, and the wider the difference between real national income and its measure in $ US per capita.[1]

But the bias is not perfectly systematic. A country, rich or poor, tends to have its price level in $ US forced down if it levies high export taxes and low import taxes, if it exports a large volume of food products, or if it has a high internal cost of transport.

Perhaps the greatest deficiency in the statistics of $ US per capita as indicators of conditions in the underdeveloped world is that they do not distinguish between countries with primitive economies and countries that are perhaps less primitive but very poor. There is reason to believe that people are very much better off in Burma than in India; I conjecture that this difference does not show up in the income statistics because India, as the more industrialised country of the two, tends to have its income in $ US buoyed up by many of the same forces that buoy up incomes in the industrial countries of Europe and America.

Difficulties in income comparisons through the foreign exchange rate have led statisticians and economists to construct comparisons between countries at a common set of prices. The numbers of loaves of bread eaten, of cars purchased, of machine tools produced, of civil servants employed, of medical services provided, of all of the items that go to make up income, are recorded and valued the same way everywhere. Ultimately this method of computing real incomes yields numbers that come closer to revealing the information we require of them. But the formulation and interpretation of these numbers involve serious statistical and conceptual problems which it is the object of this *Paper* to examine. Section II defines terms and explains what we hope to learn from statistics of real income. Sections III, IV and V take up the three main conceptual problems, the determination of the scope of income, the break-down of the flow of income into commodities, and the choice of prices. Section VI presents some results and examines some short-cut techniques.[2]

[1] Comparative price levels are less than fully reflected in the foreign exchange rate because of the way untraded products are priced and because of the effect on price levels of international and internal transport cost and of the tariff structure. P. W. Sherwood, 'Export Duties and the National Income Account', *Economic Journal*, 1956; B. Belassa, 'The Purchasing-Power Parity Doctrine: A Reappraisal', *Journal of Political Economy*, 1964; and D. Usher, 'The Transport Bias in Comparisons of National Income', *Economica*, 1963.

[2] One problem not dealt with in this *Paper* is faulty measurement. Our concern is exclusively with what to measure rather than with how to measure it, or whether it is now being measured correctly. In practice, even population statistics are subject to error, and statistics of consumption of home-grown food are often based on nothing stronger than guesses about likely consumption patterns. Methods of collecting the primary data in the national accounts are examined by Phyllis Deane, *Colonial Social Accounting*, Cambridge University Press, 1953.

# II  Definitions of Income, Real Income and Biases in the Measurement of Real Income

Income is a statistical measure, real income is a partly technical and partly psychological characteristic of an economy, and a bias in real income is a failure of a statistical measure to represent accurately what we mean by real income. Income itself is the evaluation at the going market price of a flow of goods and services in a given area and over a given period of time. In short

$$\text{Income} = \sum_i Q_i \text{ (quantity)} \times P_i \text{ (price)}$$

where the subscript $i$ refers to different types of commodities consumed and $\sum$ refers to the sum over the different commodities. Income is a statistical aggregate which may (subject to qualifications discussed below) be measured in an exact way; one finds out what has been produced and evaluates these products at market prices or at the prices they would have fetched if traded on the market.

Where income is measured for a country, it is referred to as national income. Income can be divided into sectors by areas, industries, social classes, shares of factors of production, types of commodities bought (for instance, consumption and investment), public and private, and so on.

## (a) The welfare interpretation of real income

A single income figure may stand by itself without reference to any other income figure, but the concept of real income is only relevant to comparisons. Most often, measures of real income are used as indicators of economic welfare. Welfare is a tricky concept that is better approached by welfare questions than by a formal definition. For instance, a statistician may be requested to construct a measure of the real income of India, indicating to a typical Englishman how much money he would have to possess in England to be as well off as he would be in India with a typical income there. This calculation takes account of food and clothing, board and transport but not the pleasures of living among one's own people or the happiness that one gets from meditation, etc. A distinction is sometimes drawn between economic welfare and total welfare, the former being that satisfaction one gets from goods and services that can be produced, bought and sold, and the latter satisfaction derived from all sources. Real income measures economic welfare only.[1]

A comparison of real income as economic welfare also disregards conspicuous consumption. It may be that when real income reaches a certain level further satisfaction consists only in having more than one's neighbour. Were this so, an increase in national incomes of rich countries distributed in proportion to present relative shares would make no one better off. Though the idea of conspicuous consumption is appealing, no account is taken of it in our examination of real income comparisons.

Measures of real income may represent welfare in different ways. To say that a comparison of real income is to represent welfare is not yet to provide a clear picture of what it is that is being compared. We have cited one question that a comparison of real income between Britain and India might be designed to answer. Another question that might equally fall under the heading of comparisons of real income representing economic welfare is: what income in India would make a typical Indian as well off as he would be in England with

---

[1] The use of income statistics in policy-making requires that there be a correspondence, however rough and approximate, between the numbers claimed to represent economic welfare and human happiness, total welfare, good states of consciousness or some equivalent psychological or social experience; if not, there would be no reason to seek more income rather than less. This correspondence between numbers and experience has been examined by Professor S. H. Frankel who points out several circumstances in which it may not hold.

First, income is only part of welfare and what increases income may not increase welfare if another aspect of welfare is affected adversely in the process.

'Bushmen of Social Africa remained hunters because they liked hunting; income to the Bushmen was defined in terms of success in the chase and in the sustenance yielded by the chase alone. Such income could not be compared with "equivalent" goods and services which might have resulted from some other form of activity.'

Second, the relation between economic welfare and total welfare may be such that disadvantages in the social system begin to hurt only when a degree of prosperity is attained. It is just possible that an oppressed minority may become more miserable once prosperity allows it the leisure to appreciate its situation fully.

Third, the nature and composition of economic welfare is not found, *a priori*, outside society, but is formed and determined by the institutions, laws, customs and beliefs of each society. Total welfare gives meaning to economic welfare and not the other way round. In contrast to our usual model of economic life based on cold, rational, utterly selfish 'economic man', Professor Frankel poses the analogy of economic activity as a game with income as the score: 'To identify, or seek for, a functional relationship between income and total welfare is as logically fallacious as to identify the points scored in playing a game with the "value" of the game to the players'. (' "Psychic" and "Accounting" Concepts of Income and Welfare', *Oxford Economic Papers*, 1952.)

The enterprise of comparing real national incomes—and this *Paper* is no exception—is based on the premise that economic welfare can be extricated from total welfare and analysed separately.

The use of the notion of 'a typical Englishman' in the text implies sufficient comparability in the economic welfare of different Englishmen to permit us to say whether or not Englishmen as a whole are better off. We normally say that Englishmen as a whole are better off when there has been an increase in goods and services that *could* be distributed to make each man better off, and when the pattern of income distribution has not changed very much. On alternative interpretations of community indifference curves, see Professor Paul Samuelson, 'Social Indifference Curves', *Quarterly Journal of Economics*, February 1956.

an average English income, and how does this income compare with the average Indian income? These two comparisons of Indian and British real incomes, one by English standards and the other by Indian standards, yield different results. Though the English income appears higher by both tests, it is relatively higher when viewed by Indian standards than when viewed by English standards. This proposition, which will be demonstrated in detail below (pp. 26–30), is true even if we assume that the tastes of Englishmen and Indians are exactly the same. For the present it is sufficient to note that income comparisons representing welfare involve not a single question or means of comparison but a variety of interrelated questions requiring somewhat different answers.

### (b) Other interpretations of real income

Closely allied with the welfare interpretation of real income is its interpretation as a measure of productivity. Income can be looked upon as a heap of goods, in which case one man is more productive than some other if he produces the bigger heap. Comparisons of productivity of sectors of the economy, agriculture, manufacturing, services, etc., use income per man employed as a productivity measure. The connection between the productivity and welfare interpretation of real incomes arises in the weighting of the different products; both employ prices to bring the different items onto a common scale. However commodities are normally valued at factor cost in productivity comparisons and at market prices in welfare comparisons.[1]

Statistics of real income may be constructed for special purposes, such as measuring a country's economic capacity to make or participate in war, or of ability to share in the cost of international organisations. The UN statistics were constructed partly with the latter object in mind. The military interpretation of real income approaches the fringe of the concept and it is a moot point whether flows of commodities weighted by prices chosen to reveal best the fighting capacity of a nation ought to be considered as income figures at all. Price weights used for this purpose ought to differ considerably from weights designed to reveal comparative welfare. On the other hand we must not insist on building liberal assumptions into our concepts and statistical measures. Some centralised economies are directed in a way that appears rational only if it is assumed that the object of economic activity is to maximise military capacity. Incomes might be assessed on the same criteria that economies are directed.

Finally statistics of real income, however interpreted, are used as pegs on which to hang other characteristics of the economy. It may for instance be

J. R. Hicks, 'The Valuation of Social Income', *Economica*, May 1940.

asked whether there is more equality in the distribution of income in poor countries or in rich countries, whether or to what extent economic progress increases the proportion of the labour force in manufacturing, whether rich countries grow faster than poor countries, whether consumption as a proportion of income or consumption of some variety of goods increases as a country becomes better off, whether social mobility, literacy or political freedom can be associated in any way with prosperity, and so on. To answer any of these questions requires at a minimum that a correlation be shown between statistics of real national income of different countries or of the same country over time and some other social or economic characteristics.[1]

### (c) Biases in measurement

Measures of income are adjusted in various ways to represent real income and we say that a measure is biased if it falls short of representing real income in some respect. Of course a single measure may be unbiased on one interpretation of income, and biased on another. Consequently, in evaluating measures of real income and in setting down rules for their construction, it is important to be quite clear about what real income is to represent. It is not even sufficient to say that real income represents economic welfare unless it is also specified by whose standards and under what circumstances welfare is being measured.[2]

## III  The Scope of Income

Under this heading is discussed the general problem of deciding which commodities are to be included in real income. We have in mind primarily a welfare interpretation of income on the assumption that tastes of people in the countries compared are more or less the same. To say that tastes are the same is not to say that people do consume the same things. Similarity in tastes is consistent with people in hot countries using air-conditioning and people in cold countries using heating equipment, and with people eating rice in areas suitable for rice cultivation and wheat in areas suitable for wheat cultivation. When an economist says that two people, or peoples, have the same taste he means that they would always choose the same preferred consumption pattern from among a

---

[1] An example of the use of income statistics as pegs for hypotheses is Colin Clark's claim that economic progress results in an increase in the proportion of the labour force engaged in secondary and tertiary production. See also I. B. Kravis, 'International Differences in the Distribution of Income', *Review of Economics and Statistics*, 1960; E. E. Hagen, 'Some Facts about Income Levels and Economic Growth', *Review of Economics and Statistics*, 1960; and I. Adelman and C. T. Morris, 'Factor Analyses of the Interrelationship between Social and Political Variables and Per Capita Gross National Product', *Quarterly Journal of Economics*, 1965.

[2] It is of course open to the statistician to say that he is undertaking such-and-such a calculation which the user may interpret as he pleases, but then it is open to the user to adjust the calculation to his own purposes and neither the original statistic nor the revision has any particular right to the title of *the* measure of real income.

set of alternative patterns of consumption. Similarity of taste implies like behaviour in like situations only.

Two general considerations might be emphasised before we proceed to details. The first is that any comparison ought to include the same items in both countries, 'same' being understood in an economic rather than purely technical sense. Imagine a comparison of real income between an industrial country that imports all its food and a peasant economy based on subsistence farming. A definition of income that restricted the scope of income to commodities traded on the market might be technically the same for both countries; the statistician compiling the national incomes would apply identical rules and procedures everywhere. Nevertheless the definitions of income in the two countries would be different or incongruent from an economic point of view because food is included in the definition of income in one country and excluded from the definition of income in the other.

Secondly, the choice of commodities to be included in income invariably involves a balancing of subjective and objective considerations. The requirements of the concept of real income conflict with the need for reasonably exact statistical measures that do not depend too much on the individual judgements of the statistician. Housewives' services are a case in point. The concept of income as a flow of goods and services suggests that services of housewives be included. But as there is no market setting a price for housewives' services, as we cannot say whether ₃their value should increase or decrease over time, and as there are many housewives, the decision to include their services in income might leave the all-important question of whether income is increasing or decreasing over time to the discretion of the statistician in his choice of how housewives' services are to be evaluated. Housewives' services are excluded from income because we want the comparison of incomes to be reasonably independent of the personal judgement of the statistician, and not because we believe that housewives' services ought not to be there. How far one dare go in introducing questionable items into comparisons of income depends in part on who one happens to be. The independent scholar has much more freedom in this matter than does the government statistician who, quite properly, must justify his figures by generally accepted statistical criteria.

Most of the problems we discuss under the heading of the scope of income are well-known in the literature on national accounting, as they tended to arise when the limits were first being set on the items to be included in the national accounts. Very often the choice between inclusion or exclusion of a questionable item would favour objective over subjective considerations because the really important use of the national accounts was to measure growth, and the questionable items were thought either to remain unchanged or to grow more or less at the same rate as items included in the accounts. It is different in welfare comparisons among countries with dissimilar social and economic conditions. In this problem the subjective consideration of making the statistical measures correspond to the concept of real income we have in mind might be given relatively more weight because, as we shall see, the questionable items are much less likely to remain constant in a comparison among different countries than in a comparison of incomes in one country over a relatively short period of time.

There is a standard rule in national income accounting that the national income includes all goods and services produced during the year, exclusive of intermediate products, and with allowance made for depreciation. Each of the three key terms in this rule, goods and services, intermediate products and depreciation, gives rise to a number of interesting problems and the examination of the scope of income can be sub-divided under these headings.

### (a) Goods and services

In most countries the scope of national income is not limited to commodities bought and sold. The usual practice is for some commodities not exchanged for money, because they are consumed by the producer or because they are bartered, to be included in income at imputed values. Among the imputations in the British national income are rents of owner-occupied houses and of publicly-owned buildings, farm produce consumed by the farmer, and employee's remuneration in kind like free coal for miners and food and lodging for the armed forces. Most of the national incomes of the underdeveloped countries include imputations for subsistence agriculture;[1] the statistics of value added in agriculture are compiled from estimates of total production. Recreation, funerals, religious services, domestic service and indigenous medicine, provided outside the market sector in a peasant economy and sometimes included in national income and sometimes not, ought to be fully included in a comparison with a country where these items are automatically part of income because they are within the market sector.

A case can be made for including housewives' services as part of income. There is a well-known example in economics of the man who increases national income by divorcing his wife and then hiring her as a housekeeper; the housekeeper's wage is part of income while the same service performed by a wife is not. Estimates of the value of housewives' services have occasionally been put into the national income accounts, usually in such a way that total income

---

[1] In *The Income of Nations*, p. 177, P. Studenski cites evidence that the farmer's own consumption as a percentage of total farm income was 26% in Ireland in 1953 and 18% in Canada in 1950. I estimate that the comparable figure for Thailand now is over 50%.

could be read off with or without this item. The inclusion of this item has increased income at different times and places from 10 per cent to 25 per cent.[1] As has already been mentioned, the reason for not including housewives' services in income is that this item cannot be accurately measured.

Exclusion of housewives' services probably biases down incomes of poor countries in comparison with incomes of rich countries because the definition of income includes two substitutes for housewives' services which are more plentiful in rich countries than in poor countries. The substitutes are mechanical aids to housewives (stoves, refrigerators, vacuum cleaners, washing machines) and commercial firms (laundries, milk delivery, bakeries) performing services which housewives in poor families might perform for themselves. It is not altogether certain where the balance lies because it might be argued that the substitutes for housewives' services in rich countries create better services, better food or more cleanliness, rather than merely making work easier and allowing a given real output to be produced with less expenditure of labour. But insofar as these substitutes merely generate leisure they ought to be excluded from the accounts, for leisure itself is excluded from income.

Inclusion of the substitutes for housewives' services might be justified, even when their effect is only to generate leisure, on the ground that housewives who work less are better off, that marginal increments of leisure generated in this way might be included in income even if leisure as a whole is not. There is some force in this argument when the comparison is of incomes at different times in a single country, for in such circumstances it might reasonably be supposed that housewives' hours of work would have remained unchanged but for mechanical aids and assistance from commercial firms. The argument has less force in a comparison between societies. One would not want to include a labour-saving expense as part of the income of an industrial society in a comparison with a peasant society if leisure as a whole is excluded, for the balance of leisure may, for all we know, favour the peasant society.[2]

The services of the stock of consumer durables and of public capital, roads, hospitals and public buildings, ought also to be included in a measure of real income. Some of these items are excluded because of the difficulty of measuring their contribution. The net effect of this exclusion is as a rule to bias down the incomes of rich countries especially, because typically a rich country has a

[1] Studenski, *op. cit.*, p. 177, refers to one author who, probably facetiously, goes so far as to include 'matrimonial' services rendered to each other by husband and wife on the ground that they can be substituted for by the use of paid services of male or female prostitutes. Prostitutes are excluded from income for the same reason that burglary equipment and black jacks are excluded.

[2] Leisure as a whole is excluded because of difficulties in measuring its contribution. In principle, of two countries enjoying the same flow of goods and services, we would like to say that one has a higher national income if it could get the goods and services with less expenditure of labour time.

larger capital stock (in proportion to income) of consumer durables and public goods than a poor country.

## (b) Intermediate products

A more interesting set of problems arises in the interpretation of the rule for distinguishing between final products and intermediate products. Tyres, batteries, and engine parts are sold by their manufacturers to an automobile manufacturer who assembles them into a completed car that is sold to a retailer and resold to the final consumer. The car as sold to the consumer is considered a final product and its sale is recorded as an item of income in the national accounts. Tyres, batteries and engine parts, and even the completed car as sold to the retailer, are considered intermediate products and their sales are excluded from the national accounts. The reason for making a distinction between final and intermediate products is to ensure that each item produced is included once and only once in the accounts, and not repeatedly as it is sold from firm to firm on the way to the consumer. The rule in most national accounts in the Western world is that all purchases by consumers and by government (defined exclusive of its trading activities), and purchases by firms of investment goods only are recorded as final products on the expenditure side of the national accounts, while all other transactions are excluded. Transactions in final products, other than investment goods, are identified by the agents in the transaction; a sale from a firm to a household is recorded as part of consumption in the national accounts, while a sale from one firm to another is not. The rule identifies most of the items we would like to consider as final products, but it falls short of our requirements in two opposite ways: it classifies work expenses borne by the householder as final product, and it excludes expenses by the employer for the convenience, training and safety of the employee.

Expenditure on transport to work is frequently classified as income when it ought to be cost of production. Transport to work confers no net benefit on the worker; it is a cost incurred in the process of procuring goods and services already recorded in the national accounts. The rule for distinguishing final products from intermediate products, or from costs of production, records transport to work as part of income when the worker pays for it, and as an intermediate product when the employer pays for it. An employer who arranges and pays for the transport of his workers from their homes to their place of work can increase the national income by charging them for the service and raising their wages accordingly.

Anomalies like this do not matter much when income figures are used to measure economic growth in a single country. The advantage of having an unambiguous rule for the statistician to follow far outweighs the disadvantage in this misclassification of expenditures. But the rule can be quite misleading in comparisons of real incomes between countries with vastly different social and economic characteristics. Transport to work in one's own car or by purchased transport, the accompanying inflation of site rents in cities, expenses on work clothes, blue collar or white collar, are all wholly or partly costs of production misclassified by the rule as income. The importance of these items from our point of view is that many of them are costs of production of industrial society that have no counterparts in primitive communities. Only in industrial societies do men need to travel 10 or 15 miles a day from home to work and back. Consequently failure of the conventional rule to classify these items correctly tends to create a systematic bias in the income figures, making industrial societies appear richer than they really are.

On the other hand, part of the expenditure of a rich country on transport to work represents a convenience to workers made possible by the fact that they are relatively well-off. Whether or not transport to work should be counted as a final product in a comparison between a rich country and a poor country depends on the nature of the alternative. If the alternative to riding to work is walking to work and the average distance between home and the place of work is about the same in both societies, then transport to work is a net benefit to industrial society. But if the peasant lives near his land and the separation between home and place of work is a characteristic unique to industrial society, then transport to work is a cost of production borne, like all costs of production, to reap benefits which are already recorded in the accounts.

The services of government may also be looked upon as a cost of production. By services of government we mean of course not all the activities of government, not railroads or public industry or the post office, but only those that do not yield marketable goods and services. The activities that might be excluded from income are those of Parliament, of the Ministry of Finance, of the Home Office, etc. They are excluded not because they are unproductive but because they create the social conditions necessary to the functioning of the economy; their benefits accrue in the total output of goods and services already recorded in the national accounts. Government service is like the steel that goes into an automobile; both are necessary to the automobile but neither enters directly into income.[1]

[1] An Hungarian income estimate prepared in the 1930s excluded government services on the ground that governments do not 'produce values in addition to the flow of consumers' goods, but ensure only the maintenance of the present economic and social order . . . and the present level of production'. A similar view has been expressed by S. Kusnetz and the force of the argument has been recognised by J. R. Hicks. However Professor Hicks argued that in practice one should not try to separate out intermediate products of government because 'we want to measure something and not to arrive at a figure for the national income which is what it is part of because we say it is'. The discussion is reviewed in Studenski, *op. cit.*, Chapter 14; sources of the quotations may be found there.

Instances cited so far of the failure of the conventional rule to distinguish accurately between final and intermediate products have been associated with expenditure by final consumers or government that are really costs of production, and the effect of the bias has been to make rich countries appear richer than they are. The other class of deviation from the rule tends to have the opposite effect. Expenditures by firms for the benefit and safety of employees would seem to be more prominent in the rich, industrial societies than in poor, peasant societies. Incomes in rich societies are understated if working conditions are better in rich societies than in poor, and if this difference in working conditions involves firms in expenses not recorded in the accounts under food or health. On the job training, which should appear in income under the heading of education, is missing because the worker does not pay the employer for the experience. This item may even be deducted from income, for the worker may accept a lower wage than his services could command elsewhere.

Closely related to problems arising over the distinction between final and intermediate products is the question of what to do with expenditures in one country on services that are provided free by nature in another. Heating cost is the important instance. There is no doubt that expenditure on heating, or air conditioning, belongs in income in a welfare comparison in a single country between different periods of time, for 'warmth' is unquestionably a component of welfare. But suppose an income comparison is being made between a country with an ideal climate where no heating cost is ever required, and a country where heating cost in the form of direct expenditure on fuel, warm clothing, and well-insulated housing, comprises a large proportion of income.[1] If all prices were the same in both countries, a man would prefer to live in the country with the ideal climate unless his income in the cold country were sufficiently larger than his income in the warmer country to compensate for the required heating cost. An income comparison designed to indicate the comparative welfare between these countries might exclude heating cost from the income of the cold country, because heating is a cost of production of conditions provided free by nature in the warmer country.

However one environment is rarely better than another in every respect. An environment that does not require heating may require air conditioning or special precautions against earthquakes. It is difficult to decide where the balance lies; defects may cancel out, or the environment of one country may be better on the whole than the environment of another, as in a comparison

[1] I have estimated that the total cost of keeping warm in the UK, including heating, extra clothing, and well-insulated buildings, comes to about £60 per capita per annum out of a total income of £406. See 'The Thai National Income at United Kingdom Prices', *Bulletin of the Oxford University Institute of Statistics*, 1963.

between Alaska and California. The issue is complicated by the fact that air conditioning is a luxury and heating is a necessity. The poor in Scotland spend a far larger proportion of their incomes on heating than do the poor in South East Asia and there is no doubt that life without heating in Scotland is far more difficult than life without air conditioning in South East Asia. But the very rich in South East Asia may spend as much on air conditioning as the very rich in Scotland spend on heating. The decision about whether or not to include heating and air-conditioning in an income comparison between Scotland and South East Asia may depend on whether it is the condition of the rich or the poor that is emphasised.

Industrial society requires distribution costs that are unnecessary in primitive societies. The inclusion or exclusion of these extra costs is at issue in deciding whether food produced and consumed on the farm in a peasant society should be counted in a national income comparison as equivalent to food at the farm gate or to food purchased retail in a primarily industrial country. Formal identity of the definitions of income in the two countries would have us classify food at the farm as an identical product in the two countries. But economic congruence of the definitions would have us classify food at a farm in the peasant economy with food delivered to the final consumer in the industrial country.[1]

### (c) Conventions about depreciation

Income is defined as the amount of goods and services the economy might consume during the year consistent with being as well off at the end of the year as at the beginning; by convention, investment is included net of depreciation, for we should not wish to say that a country is well-off merely because it produces a large amount of capital to replace its depreciating stock. This principle might be extended in two ways, both of which are relevant to income comparisons between rich and poor countries.

---

[1] S. Kuznets increased the pre-war national income of China from $37 to $65·5 per head by the following corrections:

(1) He magnified the part of the Chinese income associated with raw materials by the ratio of raw materials to finished products in the United States because only raw materials were included in the Chinese income, while finished products appeared in the American income, and because one way or another the Chinese raw materials had to get finished (processed, distributed, etc.) in order to be consumed.

(2) He increased the Chinese income by the proportion of services to total income in the United States; services on this calculation comprised (a) items outside the market in China but inside the market in the United States, domestic services, funerals, religion, furniture, etc., (b) banking services, (c) urban rents and transport to work, (d) government. Kuznets estimated the proportion of each of the above items that represented a net benefit to the United States in comparison with China and he used only the residual in scaling up the Chinese income. ('National Income and Industrial Structure', *Econometrica*, Supplement, July 1949.) The original Chinese estimate in dollars was that of Mr. Ta Chung Liu (*China's National Income, 1931–1936*, Brookings Institution, 1946).

First, an allowance might be made in the accounts for human depreciation, associated with the gradual ageing of the labour force. Most educational expenditure is required to maintain the general level of education and only a small proportion can be said to make the general standard of education higher at the end of the year than it was at the beginning. Virtually the whole primary and secondary education and part of university education in the rich industrial countries is thus a cost of maintenance of the stock of human capital, and only improvements in the standard or extent of education can be accounted as net final product.

Secondly, the phrase 'as well off at the end of the year as at the beginning' might be interpreted per capita instead of in total. The conventional measure of depreciation might be revised to define net investment as the excess of investment above that necessary not merely to maintain the total capital but also to preserve the proportion between the capital stock and the population. This revised convention would reveal whether or not a country is preparing to increase per capita income. For instance, if gross national product is 100, investment is 30, depreciation is 5 per cent of capital, population growth is 3 per cent, and the capital stock is 500, then the net national income and net investment computed in the usual way are 75 and 5 respectively. But a 3 per cent rate of population growth requires an increase in the capital stock of 15 in order to preserve the capital-labour ratio and keep people as well off at the end of the year as they were at the beginning. On this basis national income is only 60 and net investment is –10. There are formidable statistical obstacles in the way of this calculation because we often do not know the capital stock and because in practice the growth in income in the long run is due more to technical change than to pure investment. But income statistics prepared under present convention may show positive net investment when a country is, in fact, becoming less and less well-prepared economically as time goes on. An alternative income comparison among countries in which investment is measured net of the cost of maintaining capital per head might show which among them are really preparing to be better off in the future.

# IV Prices

A statistician comparing total or average real national incomes in two countries, having decided on the scope of income in each, must take two further decisions to complete his calculation. He must break up the income of each country into quantities of a common set of commodities, and he must choose a set of prices at which the quantities in the two countries can be compared. Since the proper choice of commodities depends to some extent on how they are to be evaluated, it is convenient to examine these two choices in reverse order, prices first on the assumption that quantities have been chosen, and then commodities and quantities.

The choice of price weights is intimately connected with the welfare question being answered in the comparisons. To ask how well-off people are in one country in comparison with people in another country is not yet to pose a question precise enough to require a ratio as an answer. This general question can be broken down into a number of more specific questions, each requiring a somewhat different answer.

Suppose an income comparison is to be made between England and South East Asia. Two distinct welfare questions are:

(1) How much money would a typical resident of England require to be as well off as he would be in South East Asia on the average income there, and how does this amount of money compare with the average income in England?

(2) How much money would a typical resident of South East Asia require to be as well off as he would be in England on the average income there, and how does this amount of money compare with the average income in South East Asia?

These two income comparisons by English and South East Asian standards respectively would each seem to govern a choice of price weights. One's first reaction to these welfare questions is to say that the comparison by English standards requires English price weights and that the comparison by South East Asian standards requires South East Asian price weights. Suppose that the difference in English and South East Asian consumption patterns is attributable entirely to the fact that the people of South East Asia who are relatively poor consume mostly necessaries—food, simple clothing, simple housing— while the people of England consume relatively much more of the luxuries— cars, TV sets, and quality products of all kinds. Faced with the same real income as the people of South East Asia, an Englishman would soon adopt their consumption pattern because he too would have to reserve his income for the necessities of life. In this case the standard of living of South East Asians could be unambiguously assessed by English standards as the value of their consumption pattern at English prices, and the simple identification of the two welfare questions with English and South East Asian price weights is correct. Pairs of ratios of real incomes of two countries valued at the two sets of relative prices are known in the literature of national accounting as 'binary comparisons'.

The identification of the two welfare questions with the two sets of price weights must be qualified in one important respect. Differences in consumption patterns may be due to differences in relative prices in the two countries as well as to differences in real incomes, and insofar as relative prices are important determinants of consumption patterns the answers to the two welfare questions require ratios of real income of the two countries that are different from and in general spanned by the binary comparisons. The value at English prices of the typical consumption pattern of South East Asia is an overstatement of the real income in South East Asia assessed by English standards, because an Englishman given enough money in England to buy the typical South East Asian consumption pattern can make himself better off than he would be in South East Asia by changing his consumption pattern, buying less of the goods that are relatively expensive in England and more of the goods that are relatively cheap.

In the limit, if relative prices alone determined the consumption patterns of the two countries, the two welfare questions would point to the same ratio of real incomes somewhere in between the binary comparisons. If real income alone determined the consumption .patterns of the two countries, the two welfare questions would be answered by the two binary comparisons. The truth normally lies between these two extremes; the answers to these two questions are distinct but the ratios of real income required by the answers are not identical to the binary comparisons, and almost always lie between them.

The relation between the welfare questions and the choice of price weights is illustrated in the remainder of this section in an extended example. The reader who is impatient with little graphs and equations might skip the example and go on to Section V (page 31).

# An example of the choice of prices

The exact relation between our welfare questions and the choice of price weights in the income comparison is illustrated in the diagram on page 27. Suppose that two types of commodities, grain and machines, are consumed in different amounts and proportions by people in two countries, A and B. Relative prices between grain and machines are assumed to be different in the two countries, for otherwise there could be no doubt about the appropriate choice of price weights in the income comparison. Tastes are initially assumed to be identical in the sense that people in either country given the same choice among alternative patterns of consumption would invariably pick the same preferred consumption pattern. This final assumption is consistent with previous assumptions that prices and consumption patterns differ between the countries as long as the economies of the countries are suited to different sorts of production.

Amounts of grain and machines are measured on the vertical and horizontal axes of the diagram on a scale of one inch to one unit of grain or one machine. Per capita consumption patterns of countries A and B are shown as points A and B. People in A consume $2\frac{1}{2}$ units of grain and $2\frac{1}{2}$ units of machines; people in B consume 2 units of grain and 1 unit of machines. The identity of tastes in A and B is reflected in a common set of 'indifference curves',[1]

of which two curves, one cutting the point A and another cutting the point B, are illustrated.

A relative price of any two commodities is the rate at which they exchange one for another. This rate is necessarily equal to the marginal rate of substitution in use between them, indicated in the diagram by the slope of an indifference curve. Relative prices of grain and manufactures at A and B may therefore be read off the diagram as the slopes of the unbroken straight lines called 'budget lines', tangent to the indifference curves at A and B. The prices are one unit of grain to five units of machines at A, and three units of grain to one unit of machines at B.

The national income associated with any consumption pattern of grain and machines and with any price ratio between them may be evaluated in units of grain and therefore measured along the vertical axis. The consumption pattern in A is assumed to be $2\frac{1}{2}$ units of grain and $2\frac{1}{2}$ units of machines, and the price ratio in A is five units of machines to one unit of grain. Consequently the national income of A (at A's prices) is three units of grain—$2\frac{1}{2}$ units of grain itself plus the grain equivalent of $2\frac{1}{2}$ units of machines, equal to one-half ($2\frac{1}{2} \times 1/5$) of one unit of grain. One gets the same result for the national income of A at prices in A by projecting the budget line of A onto the vertical axis.

---

[1] Each point on the diagram represents a consumption pattern consisting of amounts of grain and machines indicated by the projections of the point onto the vertical and horizontal axes. An indifference curve is the locus of points representing consumption patterns yielding equal degrees of satisfaction to consumers. Any point to the north east of some given point must lie on a higher indifference curve, because it represents more of both goods.

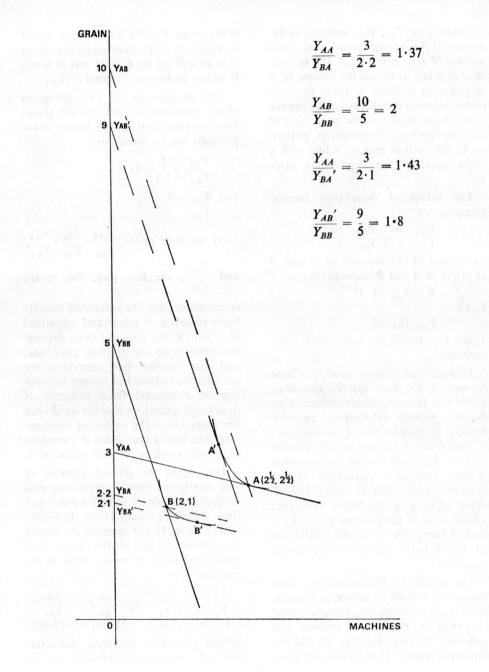

(remembering $Y_{AA}$, $Y_{BA}$, $Y_{AB}$ and $Y_{BB}$ as the incomes of ... )

$$\frac{Y_{AA}}{Y_{BA}} = \frac{3}{2\cdot2} = 1\cdot37$$

$$\frac{Y_{AB}}{Y_{BB}} = \frac{10}{5} = 2$$

$$\frac{Y_{AA}'}{Y_{BA}'} = \frac{3}{2\cdot1} = 1\cdot43$$

$$\frac{Y_{AB}'}{Y_{BB}} = \frac{9}{5} = 1\cdot8$$

Define $Y_{AA}$, $Y_{BA}$, $Y_{AB}$, and $Y_{BB}$ as the income of $A$ (in grain) at prices in $A$, the income of $B$ at prices in $A$, the income of $A$ at prices in $B$, and the income of $B$ at prices in $B$. Each of these four income measures is indicated as a distance along the vertical axis, the projection of the appropriate consumption pattern on to the vertical axis by a line with a slope equal to the appropriate price ratio.

The values of these four income measures are:

$$Y_{AA}=3 \qquad Y_{AB}=10$$
$$Y_{BA}=2\cdot2 \qquad Y_{BB}=5$$

The ratios of the incomes of $A$ and $B$ at prices in $A$ and $B$ respectively are:

$$Y_{AA}/Y_{BA}=1\cdot37$$

and

$$Y_{AB}/Y_{BB}=2$$

These two ratios are the binary comparisons.

Though each comparison is related to one of the two specific questions about real income, binary comparisons do not provide satisfactory answers, because of possibilities of substitution. A man from $A$ having enough income in $B$ to duplicate his old consumption pattern may take advantage of the different retail price to make himself better off than he was before by buying a little more of the cheaper grain at the cost of being able to afford a little less of the relatively more expensive machines.

The income in $B$ that makes a man from $A$ as well off as he was at home is not his old consumption pattern valued at prices in $B$, but an income just sufficient to keep him on his old indifference curve. This income in grain

is the point $Y_{AB}'$ on the diagram, equal to 9 units of grain. Similarly a man from $B$ is as well off in $A$ as he was at home if he has an income in grain of $Y_{BA}'$.

The answers to the two questions about comparative welfare are therefore provided not by the binary comparisons but by the ratios

$$\frac{Y_{AA}}{Y_{BA}'}=\frac{3}{2\cdot1}=11\cdot43$$

and $\dfrac{Y_{AB}'}{Y_{BB}}=\dfrac{9}{5}=1\cdot8.$

Of the four ratios, $\dfrac{Y_{AA}}{Y_{BA}}$, $\dfrac{Y_{AB}}{Y_{BB}}$, $\dfrac{Y_{AA}}{Y_{BA}'}$,

and $\dfrac{Y_{AB}'}{Y_{BB}}$, the first pair, the binary

comparisons, may be computed directly from statistics of prices and quantities in $A$ and $B$, but does not quite provide the answers to our welfare questions; and the second pair provides the answers we require but cannot in practice be computed from statistics of prices and quantities because we do not normally know the extent of substitution that would take place if a resident of $B$ were confronted with prices in $A$.

This opens the general question of how nearly the ratios representing real income comparisons as seen from $A$ and from $B$ can be estimated from the binary comparisons. In our example, the binary comparisons bracket the other two ratios and the four ratios stand in the relation

$$\underset{(1\cdot37)}{\frac{Y_{AA}}{Y_{BA}}} \leqslant \underset{(1\cdot43)}{\frac{Y_{AA}}{Y_{BA}'}} \leqslant \underset{(1\cdot80)}{\frac{Y_{AB}'}{Y_{BB}}} \leqslant \underset{(2\cdot00)}{\frac{Y_{AB}}{Y_{BB}}}.$$

Is this relation a universal characteristic of income comparisons or an accidental consequence of the numbers chosen in our example?

The first and third of these inequalities hold always because $Y_{BA}'$ is necessarily less than $Y_{BA}$ and $Y_{AB}'$ is necessarily less than $Y_{AB}$. In addition, the income of $A$ necessarily appears higher at prices of $B$ than at prices of $A$ ($Y_{AA}/Y_{BA} \leqslant Y_{AB}/Y_{BB}$), as long as each country consumes relatively more of the good that is less expensive at its own prices.

The middle inequality does not necessarily hold true in all possible circumstances, but cases in which it does hold true are of considerable practical importance. The truth or falsity of the relation

$$\frac{Y_{AA}}{Y_{BA}'} \leqslant \frac{Y_{AB}'}{Y_{BB}},$$

indicating that the income of each country appears relatively smaller when compared with the other by its own standards, depends on the reason why the two countries consume different proportions of grain and machines. As tastes are assumed to be the same, there are only two possible reasons, and they are not mutually exclusive: relatively more grain is consumed in $B$ than in $A$ either because grain is cheaper in $B$ or because poorer people consume relatively more grain than do rich people even when the relative price of grain and machines is the same to both groups. If the difference in proportions of grain and machines consumed in $A$ and $B$ is due to the first reason alone, that is to the difference in relative prices[1] exclu-

sively, then the two ratios $Y_{AA}/Y_{BA}'$ and $Y_{AB}'/Y_{BB}$ are identical and our two welfare questions yield us the same ratio of real incomes. If, on the other hand, people in $B$ would continue to consume relatively more grain than do people in $A$ even if prices were the same in both countries, if the difference in consumption patterns is what it is in part because of differences in tastes or in real income, then $Y_{AA}/Y_{BA}'$ is strictly less than $Y_{AB}'/Y_{BB}$. The point $A'$ tends to lie quite close to $A$ and the point $B'$ tends to be quite close to $B$,

so that $\dfrac{Y_{AA}}{Y_{BA}'}$ is only slightly greater

than $\dfrac{Y_{AA}}{Y_{BA}}$ and $\dfrac{Y_{AB}'}{Y_{BB}}$ is only slightly

greater than $\dfrac{Y_{AB}}{Y_{BB}}$, in which case the

relation $\dfrac{Y_{AA}}{Y_{BA}} \leqslant \dfrac{Y_{AB}}{Y_{BB}}$ ensures that $\dfrac{Y_{AA}}{Y_{BA}'}$,

$\leqslant \dfrac{Y_{AB}'}{Y_{BB}}$, be true as well. It is only when

price effects and income effects push in opposite directions that the second of the three inequalities may fail to hold.

In short the binary comparisons flank the two welfare comparisons, and each of the welfare comparisons lies closer to its corresponding binary comparison, whenever income differentials or differences in taste exert an effect on consumption patterns not counter-balanced by the effects of differences in relative prices in the countries compared. There is every reason to believe that this is

[1] In this case all indifference curves have the same shape, and the indifference curve through $B$ is a scaled-down model of the indifference curve through $A$.

generally the case in comparisons between rich and poor countries. The necessities of life—food, poor housing, clothing—are usually relatively cheap in poor countries while the luxuries—cars, radios, fine houses and clothing—consumed more by the wealthier countries are relatively dear. Incomes of the poor countries appear relatively higher by the standards of the rich countries than by the standards of the poor countries themselves.[1]

The bracketing of the true welfare comparisons by the binary comparisons is the justification for the common practice of using an average of the binary comparisons as a single welfare measure. The commonly-used statistic is the geometric average, Fisher's ideal index number, which in our example turns out to be

$$\sqrt{\frac{Y_{AA}}{Y_{BA}} \times \frac{Y_{AB}}{Y_{BB}}} = \sqrt{1 \cdot 37 \times 2} = 1 \cdot 67.$$

Suppose we want a measure representing $\frac{Y_{AA}}{Y_{BA}}$. We know that the $\frac{Y_{AA}}{Y_{BA}}$ is

an underestimate. We also know that the Fisher's index lies somewhere in the middle of the range between $\frac{Y_{AA}}{Y_{BA}}$ and $\frac{Y_{AB}}{Y_{BB}}$. The choice between $\frac{Y_{AA}}{Y_{BA}}$ and the Fisher index depends on our guess about the size of the error. We might prefer to use $\frac{Y_{AA}}{Y_{BA}}$ if we believe that the substitution effect is small in comparison with the distance between the binary comparisons. Otherwise the Fisher index is preferred.

Our example turns out to make the comparison at prices in $A$ $(1 \cdot 37)$ come out somewhat closer to the comparison of real income as seen by $A$ $(1 \cdot 43)$ than does the comparison based on the geometrical average of the binary comparisons $(1 \cdot 67)$. This is of course a consequence of the figures we have chosen and a different choice of figures could have given a different result.

[1] There is a considerable literature in economics on this point. See for instance R. Frisch, 'Annual Survey of General Economic Theory: The Problem of Index Numbers', *Econometrica*, 1936; and N. Kloek and H. Theil, 'International Comparisons of Prices and Quantities Consumed', *Econometrica*, 1965.

# V  The Choice of Quantities

Our examination of the choice of prices in the income comparison employed the working assumption that the total flows of income in the countries compared could be broken down into quantities of a common set of commodities in some obvious way. This is not always true, and in general the more different the countries compared, the more difficult it becomes to decide upon the basic quantities in the income comparison.

This difficulty is best illustrated by a comparison between a tropical country and a temperate country. Prices and quantities consumed are shown in Table II.

TABLE II

PRICES AND QUANTITIES IN A TROPICAL AND A
TEMPERATE COUNTRY

| | Tropical Country | | Temperate Country | |
| | Quantity consumed (*kilograms*) | Price (*rupees per kilogram*) | Quantity consumed (*kilograms*) | Price (*£ per kilogram*) |
|---|---|---|---|---|
| Mangos | 200 | 10 | 1 | 30 |
| Apples | 1 | 100 | 200 | 2 |
| Buffalo meat | 100 | 50 | 1 | 150 |
| Cow meat | 1 | 500 | 100 | 8 |
| Rice flour | 1,000 | 10 | 1 | 30 |
| Wheat flour | 1 | 100 | 1,000 | 1 |

The tropical country consumes relatively large amounts of tropical products, buffalo meat and rice flour, which are very cheap, and relatively small amounts of the temperate products, apples, cow meat and wheat flour, which are very expensive either because they have to be imported or because it is difficult to produce them locally. Similarly the temperate country consumes large amounts of temperate products and small amounts of tropical products. It is obvious that the binary comparisons, the two ratios of the incomes of the countries—one at the prices of the tropical country and the other at the prices of the temperate country—will be very far apart, for the income of the temperate country appears enormous at prices of the tropical country and the income of the tropical country appears enormous at prices of the temperate country.

Let $Y_{te, £}, Y_{te, R}, Y_{tr, £}, Y_{tr, R}$ be the incomes of the temperate and tropical countries expressed in pounds (the currency of the temperate country) and rupees (the currency of the tropical country). A simple manipulation of the figures in the Table indicates that

$$Y_{te, £} = £2,410 \qquad Y_{tr, £} = £51,011$$
$$Y_{te, R} = R170,070 \qquad Y_{tr, R} = R17,700$$

and that the ratios of the income of the tropical country to the income of the temperate country valued in pounds and rupees respectively are

$$\frac{Y_{tr, £}}{Y_{te, £}} = \frac{51,011}{2,410} = 21 \cdot 1$$

$$\frac{Y_{tr, R}}{Y_{te, R}} = \frac{17,700}{170,070} = \cdot 104$$

In this example, the income of the tropical country is either 20 times that of the temperate country or only one-tenth depending on which set of price weights is used!

Real income might have been calculated in a different way. Suppose that, instead of accepting the commodities in detail as the basic units of the comparison, we had initially decided to use only fruit, meat and flour as commodity units and to price them at unit values in each country. Table II is now compressed to the form shown in Table III.

TABLE III

THE COMMODITIES COMPRESSED*

| | Tropical Country | | Temperate Country | |
| | Quantity consumed (kilograms) | Price (rupees per kilogram) | Quantity consumed (kilograms) | Price (£ per kilogram) |
|---|---|---|---|---|
| Fruit | 201 | 10·4 | 201 | 2·1 |
| Meat | 101 | 54·5 | 101 | 9·4 |
| Flour | 1,001 | 10·1 | 1,001 | 1·0 |

* The prices are calculated by dividing the total value of the items included in the Table by the total quantity. For example, the total quantity of fruit in the tropical country is 201 kilos, 200 of mangos and 1 of apples. The total value is 2,100 rupees, 200 kilos of mangos at ten rupees per kilo plus 1 kilo of apples at 100 rupees per kilo. The unit value of a kilo of fruit is 10·4 rupees (2,100/201) per kilo.

A glance at Table III reveals that this revised calculation makes the real incomes of the two countries equal because all quantity units are the same in each country. The Fisher index of the average of the binary comparisons taken from Table II gives a different result; the geometric average of the binary comparisons, 21·1 and ·104, gives the impression that the real income of the tropical country is about half as much again as the real income of the temperate country. We have of course concocted this example to make the comparison in terms of a few common, in a sense artificial, commodities appear right, while the binary comparisons based on a detailed enumeration of commodities, and the geometric average of the binary comparisons, appear wrong on almost any interpretation of income as a welfare measure. A different example could have yielded a different result. In particular the choice of common commodities is rarely as easy as in our example.

As much as he dislikes imposing his own judgements on the data, the statistician cannot avoid having to choose a common set of commodities, for in principle and possibly even in practice there is no limit to the extent of subdivision of commodities. We started out the example as if all mangos, apples, cow meat, etc., were homogeneous. This in itself would require a judgement about the comparability of grades of meat, and of sizes and varieties of mangos or apples, etc. As a rule the appropriate degree of detail in specification of commodities depends on the similarity of the countries. A comparison of incomes of the United States and European countries can withstand quite a fine breakdown of incomes without creating a vast dispersion in the results of the binary comparisons. An attempt to compare the income of a European country with that of an agricultural country in the tropics could yield results like that in our example unless the number of commodities were kept to a minimum.[1]

There is a close connection between the choice of items to be subsumed under a single commodity in an income comparison and the problem of balancing off substitution effects and income effects in the choice of price weights. Items are treated as units of the same commodity if they are close substitutes, in the special sense that the consumption of each good would be sensitive to changes in the price of the other if both goods were plentiful. When these potential substitutes are put separately into income, the substitution effect in the comparison at one set of prices becomes very large. The substitution effect is reduced greatly by amalgamating potential substitutes into common commodities.

[1] S. Kuznets has expressed the hope that the choice of commodities could ultimately be made on scientific principles: 'The eventual solution would obviously lie in deriving a single yardstick that would be applied to both types of economies—a yardstick that would perhaps be outside the different economic and social institutions and would be grounded in experimental science (of nutrition, warmth, health, shelter, etc.)'. ('National Income and Industrial Structure', *Econometrica*, Supplement, 1949, p. 225.)

An Englishman disposing aid may want a measure of income indicating how much it would cost in England to buy a bundle of goods (the cheapest) that would make an Englishman as well off as a typical resident of some underdeveloped country. The best indicator for this problem might be one at British prices with large substitutions allowed for in the choice of commodities; underdeveloped fruit would be equated by weight or calorific equivalence to British fruit, underdeveloped fish equated to British fish, and so on. The fact that the British income looks enormous to the resident of the underdeveloped country because cars, radios, TV sets, are very expensive (and very rare) in the underdeveloped country is largely irrelevant to the purpose of this comparison. The statistician from the underdeveloped country who wants to know how well off the British are by his standards will evaluate commodities differently. An international organisation trying somehow to satisfy both parties may take an average of the comparisons computed from the two points of view.

## VI  Systems of Measurement

(a) *Income comparisons among countries at common prices*

The earliest attempt to compute the national incomes of many countries at a common set of prices was that of Colin Clark. He employed as weighting systems what he called 'oriental units' representing the purchasing power of a rupee in India, and 'international units' representing the purchasing power of a US dollar.[1]

Comparisons of the real incomes of the United States and several European countries at American and 'average European' prices were prepared by M. Gilbert and I. Kravis under the auspices of the OECD.[2] Some results of this study together with comparisons between the United States and China and between the United States and the Soviet Union are presented in Table IV. The different figures are not entirely comparable, because they have been compiled at different times, by different people and for different purposes; they are placed together in the Table to illustrate the orders of magnitude. Without exception the real incomes of all the countries, except of course the United States, appear larger at American price weights than at local price weights. All the real incomes appear larger in relation to that of the United

---

[1] *The Conditions of Economic Progress*, Macmillan, 1940.

[2] Previously the International Labour Office had performed similar computations in measuring costs of living in different countries. H. Staehle, *International Comparisons of Food Costs*, ILO, 1934. This work includes references to older literature on the subject.

States when measured at a common set of price weights than when measured by dividing national income in the local currency by the foreign exchange rate between the local currency and US dollars.

TABLE IV

REAL NATIONAL INCOMES PER HEAD EXPRESSED AS
PERCENTAGES OF THE REAL INCOME PER HEAD
OF THE UNITED STATES

| | (1) | (2) | (3) | (4) |
|---|---|---|---|---|
| | Ratios of incomes in local currencies weighted by the foreign exchange rate between the local currency and $ US | at US prices | at local prices | Geometric average of (2) and (3) |
| UK (1955) | 42 | 64 | 51 | 57 |
| France (1955) | 47 | 56 | 43 | 49 |
| Italy (1955) | 19 | 35 | 24 | 29 |
| USSR (1955) | — | 45 | 22 | 31 |
| China (1952) | 2·5 | 6·1 | 1·8 | 3·3 |

*Sources:* The estimates for the UK, France and Italy are from M. Gilbert and Associates, *Comparative National Products and Price Levels*, OECD, Paris, 1958, Table 4, p. 28. The estimates for the USSR are from *Comparisons of United States and Soviet Economies*, Joint Economic Committee, Congress of the United States, 1959. The estimates for China are from W. W. Hollister, *China's Gross National Product and Social Accounts 1950–1957*, Free Press, Glencoe, Ill., 1958.

The comparison between China and the United States in Table IV is only one of many attempts to compare national incomes of developed and underdeveloped countries. M. F. Millikan has estimated that the real incomes of many African and Asian countries are 350 per cent larger than indicated by the UN statistics of national income in $ US per capita, and E. E. Hagen has estimated that the comparable figure for Burma is over 300 per cent.[1] I have estimated that the ratio of British to Thai national income per head is 13·06 when incomes in local currencies are converted to pounds by the foreign exchange rate, 6·27 when both incomes are valued at Thai prices, and 2·76 when both incomes are valued at British prices.

The nature of the problems that arise in comparing national incomes at a common set of prices in a wealthy industrial economy and a poor peasant

[1] Both estimates are cited in C. Kindleberger, *Economic Development*, McGraw-Hill, 1958, Chapter 1.

economy may be seen in magnification by considering the item in the national accounts that is least comparable from one country to the next. All three of the general problems we have been examining, the scope of income, prices, and commodities make their appearance in evaluating the services of housing.

The typical farm-house in South East Asia is a platform raised from the ground on stilts, and covered by a roof made of leaves. The walls are thatched and the house is usually divided into several rooms. There is no running water but this is not as severe an inconvenience as it would be in England because the climate is always warm and there are usually streams nearby.

What in England might the typical South East Asian farm-house be compared with? Should a statistician comparing incomes inquire from a British builder what it would cost to construct such a house in England? If so, how should the site rent be valued? Should the hut be built in the Lake District or, since most Englishmen have to live in cities, in the centre of London? A more important consideration is that the English climate would make living in such a house very much more unpleasant in England than in South East Asia. A comparable house would have at least to include some provision for heating.

The question of heating cost takes us back to the determination of the scope of income. To decide as one might that a South East Asian farm-house is to be equated to a given standard of housing in England plus a given level of heating cost is implicitly to postulate that heating is to be counted as an intermediate product and not as a final product in this context. Every comparison of real income, implicitly or explicitly, requires a judgement equating housing standards. The UN method of expressing incomes in $ US per capita postulates in effect that housing standards in the countries compared are proportional to values of housing expressed in $ US. In my comparison of the incomes of Thailand and the UK, I did not even try to find an objective measure of housing services and simply assumed that people in the UK are twice as well housed as people in Thailand. Gilbert and Kravis were able to get direct measures of housing services in Europe and the United States.

## (b) *The social adequacy method*

The direct comparison of incomes evaluated at a common set of prices is often laborious and invariably subject to the judgement of the statistician making the comparison. There are a number of short-cut methods which we shall now examine. The UN method has been discussed in the introduction and need not be taken up again now.

A rough measure of welfare cutting out most of the pricing problems we have examined can be obtained by expressing incomes as multiples of the subsistence level. In each country income per head in local currency is divided by an estimate of the bare cost of subsistence; ratios arrived at in this way are then treated as measures of real income. The one attempt to compare incomes by this method,[1] a comparison of Japan and the United States, raised the ratio of the Japanese to the American income almost 600 per cent over what it appears to be when national incomes are compared through the foreign exchange rate.

There are a number of difficulties with this type of comparison that considerably limit the usefulness of the results. First, as there is no firm line of division between an adequate and an inadequate income, the choice of subsistence incomes in the countries compared, and consequently the results of the comparison, depend in a fundamental way on the judgement of the statistician making the comparison. Governments compute estimates of income necessary for an adequate standard of living, but there is no assurance that these statisticians will be comparable from one country to the next. It often turns out that people in rich countries suppose the minimum subsistence income to be relatively high, while people in poor countries suppose the minimum subsistence income to be relatively low.

Second, among countries that are well above subsistence, it may happen that one has an income which is the larger multiple of the subsistence level while another is actually better off because prices of goods bought in addition to what is needed merely to subsist are relatively lower. The author cited as using this method was aware of both of these defects and intended his results as a complement rather than a substitute for other methods.

### (c) Direct attempts to measure levels of living

Several attempts have been made to simplify international comparisons of welfare by expressing welfare in terms of one or more key indicators chosen either because they represent an important component of welfare or because they are thought to be correlated with income as a whole. The simplest and in some respects most useful indicators of this type are 'grain equivalents'; national income, or some part of it—consumption, wages or agricultural output—may be compared in grain equivalents by dividing money values by the grain prices. The representation of wages in kilos of grain has a good deal in common with the social adequacy method of income comparison because the minimum subsistence income is often closely related to grain price. Though this measure suffers from many of the same defects as the social adequacy

[1] A. H. Gleason, 'The Social Adequacy Method of International Level of Living Comparisons as Applied to Japan and the United States', *The Journal of Economic Behaviour*, April 1961.

method, it can be used with some effect to show the standard of living of the poor.[1]

A natural extension of this method that is still short of a full comparison of national income is to measure standards of living by a weighted average of a number of quantities of goods and services produced or consumed.[2] The difficulty with this type of comparison is that of knowing how to weight the different indices in the final comparison. A weighting that emphasises agricultural production or food consumption tends to overstate the incomes of the poorer countries, while a weighting that emphasises industrial products—radios, cars, and the like—tends to overstate the incomes of the richer countries. The problem is analogous to that discussed above of choosing price weights in a full income comparison, except that it is compounded by the need to choose quantities as well.

### (d) Projections

Measures of real income are often correlated with other social or economic characteristics of countries to reveal structural similarities or dissimilarities. Relations of this type can also be used to estimate real national incomes in countries where full data required for measuring real income are not available.

If real incomes are known for some countries but not for others, it is possible to estimate real incomes of the other countries by correlating data on real income with other social facts on which data is available in many countries, and then using the correlation to obtain real incomes in the remainder of the countries.

The method of projections was first used to correct the United Nations figures of national income in US dollars per capita estimated through the foreign exchange rate, in the light of direct comparisons of incomes at common prices. The UN figures are available for many countries; direct comparisons are available for only a few. It was found that, among countries where both types of national income comparison were available, the rankings of countries on the scale of rich and poor were about the same in the two methods of comparison, but the absolute values differed considerably; the ratio of highest to lowest income was far larger in the UN comparison than in the direct comparison. The direct comparison was believed to be correct, and a correction factor was applied to the UN comparison. Incomes were raised by different proportions depending on their place on the scale; lowest incomes were raised most, medium incomes were raised less and the very highest income was raised

---

[1] 'Agricultural Progress Measured in Grain Equivalents', Chapter IV of C. Clark and M. R. Haswell, *The Economics of Subsistence Agriculture*, Macmillan, 1964.

[2] M. K. Bennett, 'International Disparities in Consumption Levels', *American Economic Review*, September 1951.

not at all. The extent of the correction was chosen to make the spread between high and low incomes about the same in the direct comparison at a common set of prices and in the UN comparison altered in this way. Applying this technique, J. P. Delahaut and E. S. Kirschen[1] concluded that national incomes per capita of less than $50 US as estimated by the UN ought on the average to be increased by 211 per cent.

The technique has been extended by W. Beckerman[2] who based income projections on economic indicators like tons of steel consumed and numbers of letters despatched rather than on the UN figures. A relationship, found to hold between real incomes assessed by direct comparisons at common prices and a set of economic indicators, was used to estimate real incomes of countries for which direct comparisons are not available.

Projections may be labour-saving and they may reveal useful facts about recurrent patterns of economic behaviour in different countries, but they do not in any respect solve or circumvent the many conceptual problems discussed above. First, the projections are never perfect. Invariably a relation between real income and other variables is statistical, probabilistic and subject to a margin of error. We cannot know how close a projection is to the true figure until the true figure has been calculated. Second, the projections computed so far do not lend themselves to the breakdown of real income into sectors like industries, final uses or earnings of different social groups. Third, and most important, a projection requires something to project from. Initially there must be a set of real incomes which we choose to call 'correct', and from which we estimate relations for projecting other incomes. All of the conceptual problems discussed above enter into the projections in the way the initial 'correct' incomes are chosen. If the manner of measuring the 'correct' incomes of, for instance, certain underdeveloped countries in the tropics is such as to make these incomes appear high, then high incomes will be projected onto other underdeveloped countries in the tropics. This kind of problem might be partially overcome by restricting the initial 'correct' incomes to industrial countries with quite similar social and economic structures, but only at the cost of having to assume without evidence that relations observed among these countries apply to all other countries everywhere. Ultimately a projection is not an independent system of income measurement on a par with those we have been discussing. It is instead a mixture of hypotheses about similarities among the economies of different countries, and a way of guessing some incomes from others.

[1] 'Les revenus nationaux de monde non communiste', *Cahiers Economiques de Bruxelles*, No. 10, April 1961.
[2] *International Comparisons of Real Incomes*, OECD, 1966.

# VII Conclusion

One of the main themes of this *Paper* has been the view that the national incomes of poor, underdeveloped countries in US dollars per head must be very much larger than the UN figures would lead us to believe. Does this mean that people in these countries are better off than we had imagined? Paradoxically the answer to this question is that it does not. To say that widely-used estimates of the real national incomes are gross underestimates is not to say that people in underdeveloped countries are more prosperous than had been supposed. The grain ships bound for India and the reports of refugees in Hong Kong attest to the true situation in at least part of the underdeveloped world. Anyone who was led by the UN figures to believe that people in underdeveloped countries were performing the impossible by subsisting on no more than could be bought in the United States for 11 cents a day, might revise his opinions in the light of better statistics. However, the main effect of better statistics is not to make us change our views about the extent of poverty in the underdeveloped countries, but rather to make us attach different numbers to the scale of poverty and wealth.

The method of comparing incomes at a common set of prices yields statistics of national income per head that are at least not an affront to common sense, and are consistent with our knowledge of human physiology and of the general economic conditions. The removal of the absurdity in the national income statistics has not been without cost. The UN method of comparing incomes through the foreign exchange rate had the virtue that everyone using it got the same result. A comparable degree of objectivity is unobtainable when incomes are compared at a common set of prices, for there is a wide range within which reasonable men may disagree about the magnitudes. This is unavoidable if we are to measure real incomes at all. As we insist on attaching numbers to degrees of poverty and prosperity, and it is hard to imagine how we might conduct discussions about economic growth or foreign aid if we do not, we have no choice but to construct the figures as best we can, fully recognising the nature of the judgement involved.

Judgements about real incomes are, as Keynes once said of the cost of living, like historical statements such as that Victoria was a good queen but not a wise one. Our subject lies on the borderlines between science and opinion. Careful reasoning and statistical technique can refine our judgements and reduce the extent of subjectivity in them, but they cannot do away with subjectivity altogether. We cannot even in principle measure real income in the exact and unambiguous way that we measure the density of a metal or the speed of light.

# Note on Further Reading

Two good, short introductions to national income are Richard and Giovanni Stone, *National Income and Expenditure* (Bowes and Bowes, London, 1961), and H. C. Edey and A. T. Peacock, *National Income and Social Accounting* (Hutchinson's University Library, 1954). P. Studenski, *The Income of Nations* (New York University Press, 1958), consists of a history of national accounting, an excellent examination of conceptual problems in the construction and interpretation of national income statistics, and a detailed country-by-country description of methods of compilation. It is however weak on social accounting, a deficiency that can be made up by reading I. Ohlsson, *On National Accounting* (National Institute of Economic Research, Stockholm, 1953, reprinted 1961) or G. Stuvel, *System of Social Accounting* (Oxford University Press, 1965).

R. and N. D. Ruggles, *National Income Accounts and Income Analysis* (McGraw-Hill, 1956) and M. Bailey, *National Income and the Price Level* (McGraw-Hill, 1962) are studies of national accounts with special reference to Keynesian theory and the maintenance of full employment. The material in the Ruggles' book should be mastered before Bailey's book is attempted. The British student of national accounting should acquaint himself with the Blue Book, *National Income and Expenditure* (HMSO, published annually) and the explanation of how it was compiled, *National Income Statistics, Sources and Methods* (HMSO, 1956).

Turning from national income generally to the problems discussed in this *Paper*, a good deal can be learned from C. Clark, *The Conditions of Economic Progress* (Macmillan, 1940, Second Edition 1951). M. Gilbert and I. B. Kravis, *An International Comparison of National Products and the Purchasing Power of Currencies* (OECD, 1954) is an exemplary study of how to compare national incomes by revaluing them at a common set of prices. Many of the issues raised in this *Paper* are discussed in greater detail in S. Kuznets, 'National Income and Industrial Structure' (*Econometrica*, Supplement, 1949), and in M. Gilbert (ed.), *Income and Wealth*, Series III (Bowes and Bowes, 1953).

# Hobart Papers in Print

*All Capitalists Now* GRAHAM HUTTON (2*s.* 6*d.*)

1. *Resale Price Maintenance* B. S. YAMEY (fourth edition, 6*s.* max.)
2. *To Let ?* NORMAN MACRAE (3*s.* 6*d.*)
3. *Balance-sheet for Take-overs* ANTHONY VICE (3*s.* 6*d.*)
4. *Pensions for Prosperity* ARTHUR SELDON (3*s.* 6*d.*)
5. *Anything but Action ?* A. P. HERBERT (3*s.* 6*d.*)
6. *Unions in Prosperity* FRANK BEALEY and STEPHEN PARKINSON (3*s.* 6*d.*)
7. *Company Law for Shareholders* GUY NAYLOR (3*s.* 6*d.*)
13. *A Prosperous Press* IAN COLQUHOUN (5*s.*)
15. *TV: From Monopoly to Competition/and Back ?* WILFRED ALTMAN DENIS THOMAS and DAVID SAWERS (second edition, 7*s.* 6*d.*)
16. *Ordinary Shares for Ordinary Savers* RICHARD KELLETT (5*s.*)
18. *The Wage Fixers* HENRY SMITH (5*s.*)
19. *Libraries: Free-for-All ?* A. P. HERBERT (6*s.*)
21. *Freedom for Fuel* GEORG TUGENDHAT (7*s.* 6*d.*)
22. *Farming for Consumers* GRAHAM HALLETT and GWYN JAMES (6*s.*)
23. *Transport for Passengers* JOHN HIBBS (7*s.* 6*d.*)
24. *Prices for Primary Producers* SYDNEY CAINE (second edition, 7*s.* 6*d.*)
25. *Education for Democrats* A. T. PEACOCK and JACK WISEMAN (6*s.*)
26. *Taxmanship* COLIN CLARK (6*s.*)
27. *Monetary Policy for Stable Growth* E. VICTOR MORGAN (5*s.*)
28. *Vacant Possession* JOHN CARMICHAEL (6*s.*)
29. *Policy for Incomes ?* F. W. PAISH and JOSSLEYN HENNESSY (second edition, 6*s.*)
30. *Land in the Market* D. R. DENMAN (4*s.*)
31. *Money in the International Economy* GOTTFRIED HABERLER (6*s.*)
32. *Taxing Inheritance and Capital Gains* C. T. SANDFORD (6*s.*)
33. *Paying for Parking* G. J. ROTH (6*s.*)
34. *Fuller Employment ?* M. J. FARRELL (7*s.* 6*d.*)
35. *Growth through Competition* 'SPARTACUS' (7*s.* 6*d.*)
36. *Telephones—Public or Private?* MICHAEL CANES (7*s.* 6*d.*)
37. *The Company, the Shareholder and Growth* F. R. JERVIS (7*s.* 6*d.*)

*For further information about the* HOBART *and other* PAPERS, *details of subscription services, etc., please write to the IEA at*
Eaton House, 66a Eaton Square, London, S.W.1

# Eaton Papers

1. *Disclosure in Company Accounts* HAROLD ROSE (second edition, 10s. 6d. board covers, 6s. paper).
2. *Macro-Economic Models: Nature, Purpose and Limitations* MALCOLM FISHER (out of print)
3. *The Rôle of Trading Stamps in Retail Competition* CHRISTINA FULOP (7s. 6d.)
4. *The National Plan: A preliminary assessment* JOHN BRUNNER (second edition, 6s.)
5. *The Corporation Tax—a Closer Look* JOHN CHOWN (6s.)
6. *Lessons from Central Forecasting* DUNCAN BURN, J. R. SEALE and A. R. N. RATCLIFF (7s. 6d.)
7. *Wages—Fog or Facts ?* DAVID LAYTON (7s. 6d.)
8. *Cost-Benefit Analysis and Public Expenditure* G. H. PETERS (7s. 6d.)

# Occasional Papers

1. *The Intellectual and the Market Place* GEORGE J. STIGLER (1s.)
2. *Growth, Advertising and the Consumer* RALPH HARRIS (2s.)
3. *Monopoly or Choice in Health Services?* A SYMPOSIUM (5s.)
4. *Advertising and Competition* LESTER G. TELSER (6s.)
5. *Competition in Radio* DENIS THOMAS (second edition, 3s.)
6. *The Future of Steel* DUNCAN BURN and others (6s.)
7. *The Inconsistencies of the National Health Service* J. M. BUCHANAN (3s.)
8. *Economics, Business and Government* JOHN JEWKES, SIR PAUL CHAMBERS, LORD ROBBINS (5s.)
9. *Two Views on Aid to Developing Countries* BARBARA WARD and P. T. BAUER (7s. 6d.)
10. *Markets and the Franchise* T. W. HUTCHISON (6s.)
11. *After the Boom* SIR JOHN HICKS (3s. 6d.)
12. *Financing University Education* A. R. PREST (3s.)

# Research Monographs

1. *Restrictive Practices in the Building Industry* FRANK KNOX and JOSSLEYN HENNESSY (7s. 6d.)
2. *Economic Consequences of the Professions* D. S. LEES (7s. 6d.)
3. *A Self-financing Road System* G. J. ROTH (10s. 6d.)
4. *Marketing for Central Heating* CHRISTINA FULOP and RALPH HARRIS (6s.)
5. *Private Enterprise and Public Emulation* MARIO DEAGLIO (6s.)
6. *John Stuart Mill's Other Island: A study of the economic development of Hong Kong* HENRY SMITH (5s.)

USHER.    Rich and poor countries